LEARN ALL MALAYALAM ALPHABETS IN AUSTRALIA

Written & Illustrated by
DR. ABRAHAM THOMAS EETTICKAL

A COMPLETE MALAYALAM ALPHABET LEARNING GUIDE IN AUSTRALIA

VOWELS 1

A

Colour In

A-mma Mother

I love my AMMA b'cos....

ആ . . . .
A

ആ . . . .
A

ആ . . . .
A

Aa

Colour In

ആസ്ട്രേലിയ Australia

ആ.- Aa
ആ... Aa

A giant boulder fell on my leg & I screamed in pain..!

ആ . . . .
Aa
ആ . . . .
Aa
ആ . . . .
Aa

LIGHT AUSTRALIA

E

Colour In

ഇഗുവാന   Iguana

I kicked the ball and …

ഇ E . . . .

ഇ E . . . .

ഇ E . . . .

Ee

Colour In

ഈമു
Emu

Can you tell me the story of the EMU who trained to fly...

ഈ . . . .
Ee

ഈ . . . .
Ee

ഈ . . . .
Ee

LIGHT AUSTRALIA

U

Colour In

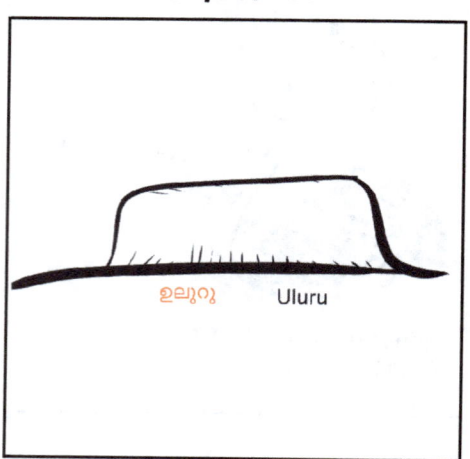

LIGHT AUSTRALIA

Uu

ഊണ് Uu-nu Meal

The best thing about the UUNU is the pappad!

ഊ . . . .
Uu

ഊ . . . .
Uu

ഊ . . . .
Uu

LIGHT AUSTRALIA

Eru

Colour In

ဥတု Ri-tu Seasons

Eru

Eru

Eru

Ae

Colour In

എക്കിഡ്ന
Echidna

I love burnt marshmallows

എി ....
Ae

എി ....
Ae

എി ....
Ae

 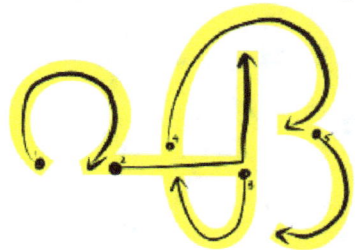

Aae

Colour In

ഏണി   Aa-ni Ladder

Days I climb and days I fly…

Aae ....

Aae ....

Aae ....

LIGHT AUSTRALIA

ഐ ഐ

Colour In

ഐസിപോൾ Icy pole

I can have a truck load of this...

ഐ ....
ഐ ....
ഐ ....

LIGHT AUSTRALIA

ഒ

Colour In

ഒപ്പറ ഹൗസ്   Opera House

A world wonder! It is massive...

LIGHT AUSTRALIA

 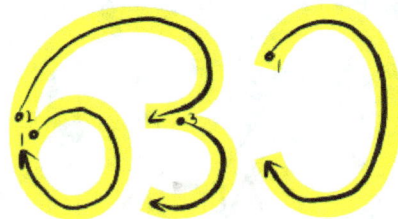

Oo

Colour In

ഓസി Aussie

Mate, I was chilling out in the bush and….

ഓ
Oo

ഓ
Oo

ഓ
Oo

LIGHT AUSTRALIA

Au

Colour In

ഔട്ട്ബാക്ക്
Outback

Where am I ?

ഔ
Au ....

ഔ
Au ....

ഔ
Au ....

LIGHT AUSTRALIA

Aam

Colour In

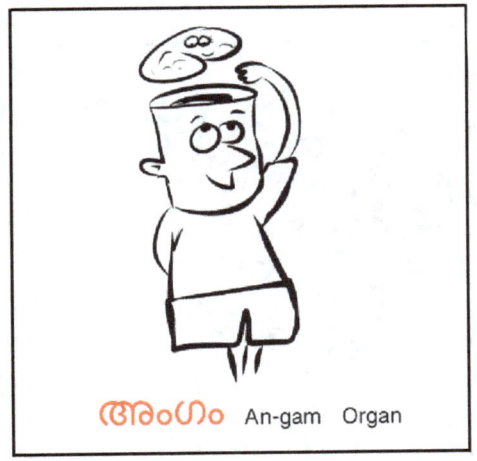

അംഗം An-gam Organ

This is the cleverest angam of my body..

Aaa

LIGHT AUSTRALIA

CONSONANTS

15

Ka

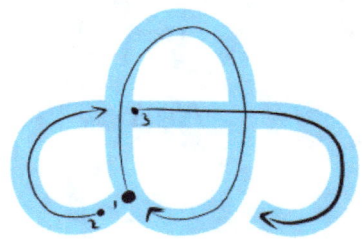

Ka

Colour In

കോല Koala

I climbed the gum tree and saw....

 Ka . . . .

 Ka . . . .

 Ka . . . .

LIGHT AUSTRALIA

16

Kha

Kha

Colour In

முகம்   Mu-kham   Face

My MUKHAM looks good…

வ........................
Kha

வ........................
Kha

வ........................
Kha

LIGHT AUSTRALIA

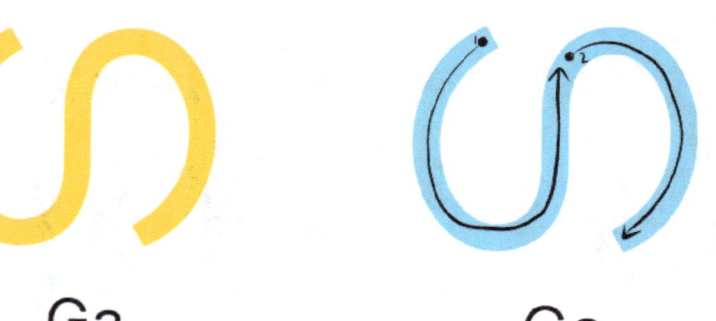

Ga　　　　　　　　Ga

Colour In

ဂုံ ရီ   Gum tree

I love my gum tree

ဂ . . . .
Ga

ဂ . . . .
Ga

ဂ . . . .
Ga

LIGHT AUSTRALIA

Gha   Gha

Colour In

മേഘം Me-kham Cloud   I love to rain…

. . . .
Gha

. . . .
Gha

. . . .
Gha

Nja

Nja

Colour In

The-nga Coconut

I am super soft inside....

LIGHT AUSTRALIA

Cha

Colour In

ചാടി Cha-di Jump

No one can beat me in this….

 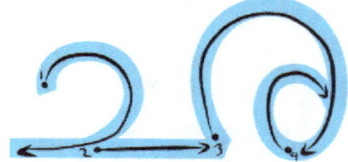

Chha

Colour In

ഛായ   Cha-ya   Likeness

LIGHT AUSTRALIA

Ja

Colour In

Ja-yam Victory

I was about to win… then….

Tha

Colour In

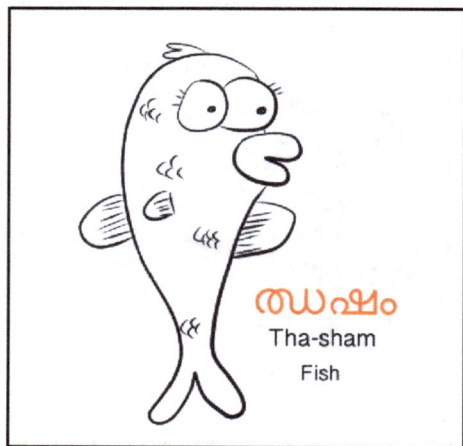

തധഷം
Tha-sham
Fish

There is something fishy

തധ ....
തധ ....
തധ ....

LIGHT AUSTRALIA

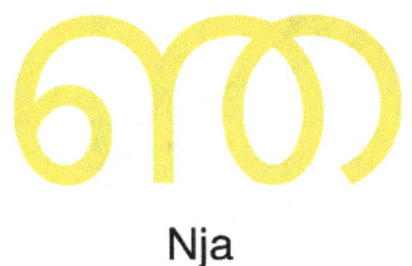 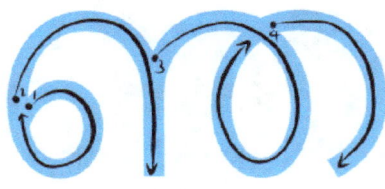

Nja

Colour In

ഞാൻ Nj-an Me

ഞ ....
ഞ ....
ഞ ....

Tah

Tah

Colour In

ടാസി ഡെവിൾ
Tassie devil

I was having my brekkie and suddenly…

LIGHT AUSTRALIA

Tha

Tha

Colour In

LIGHT AUSTRALIA

27

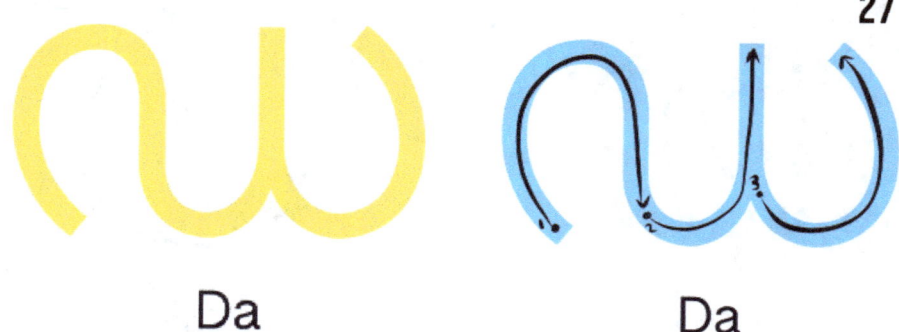

Da   Da

Colour In

ဍာန်စ်
Dance

ဍ
Da ....

ဍ
Da ....

ဍ
Da ....

LIGHT AUSTRALIA

Edha   Edha

Colour In

വിഡ്ഢി   Vi-ddi   Fool

Edha ....

Edha ....

Edha ....

LIGHT AUSTRALIA

29

ങ **Nah**   ങ **Nah**

Colour In

പണം Pa-nam Money

I am rich of...

ങ . . . .
Nah

ങ . . . .
Nah

ങ . . . .
Nah

LIGHT AUSTRALIA

30

Ta

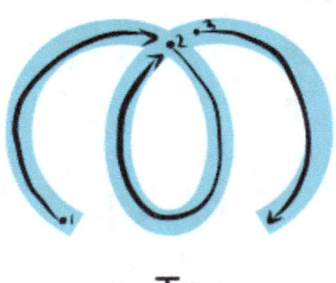
Ta

Colour In

മുതല   Mu-ta-la   Crocodile

It is not crocodile tears
I am really sad

Ta . . . .

Ta . . . .

Ta . . . .

LIGHT AUSTRALIA

 Etha

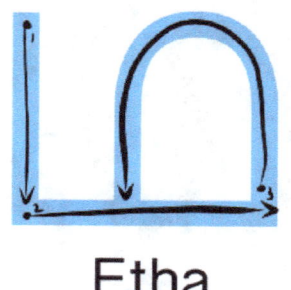 Etha

Colour In

Ka-etha Story

Etha ....

Etha ....

Etha ....

Da

Da

Colour In

Da-ya Kindness

ß
Da . . . .

ß
Da . . . .

ß
Da . . . .

LIGHT AUSTRALIA

Dha

Dha

Colour In

ഡം Dha-nam Wealth

I have lots of money

ഡ Dha . . . .

ഡ Dha . . . .

ഡ Dha . . . .

LIGHT AUSTRALIA

Na

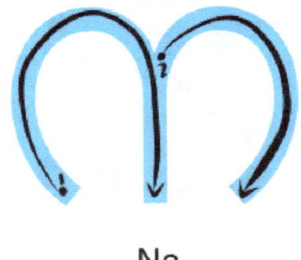
Na

Colour In

നാക്ക് Na-kku Tongue

My long Nakku is handy for

ൎ ....
Na

ൎ ....
Na

ൎ ....
Na

LIGHT AUSTRALIA

Pa

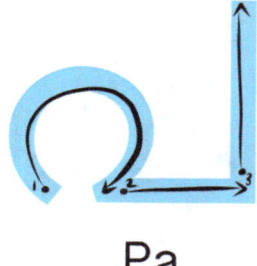
Pa

Colour In

പണം Pa-nam Money

I am rich of...

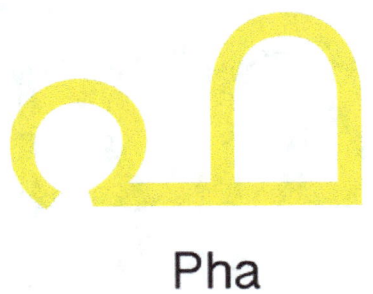
Pha

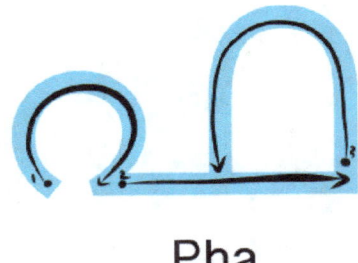
Pha

Colour In

Pha-lam Fruit

I love my fruit...

Pha ....

Pha ....

Pha ....

LIGHT AUSTRALIA

Ba

Ba

Colour In

ബിൽബി
Bilby

I was tiptoeing in the dark and….

..................................

..................................

ബ..................................
Ba

LIGHT AUSTRALIA

Bhha   Bhha

Colour In

Bha-yam Fear   I am scared of ghosts

Bhha . . . .

Bhha . . . .

Bhha . . . .

LIGHT AUSTRALIA

Ma

Ma

Colour In

മുയൽ Mu-yal Rabbit

You can't catch me
Na...na...naah...

LIGHT AUSTRALIA

40

Ya

Ya

Colour In

ယာတြာ Ya-tra Journey

I love to travel to…

ယာ ....
Ya

ယာ ....
Ya

ယာ ....
Ya

LIGHT AUSTRALIA

Ra

Ra

Colour In

LIGHT AUSTRALIA

La

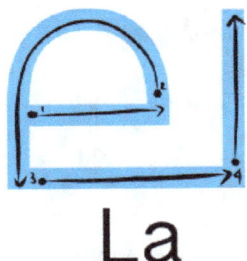
La

Colour In

Ma-la Mountain

I can move mountains

. . . .
La

. . . .
La

. . . .
La

Va

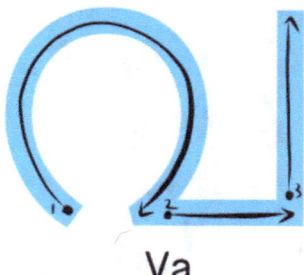
Va

Colour In

വോമ്പാറ്റ് Wombat

I love skiing....

വ ....
Va

വ ....
Va

വ ....
Va

LIGHT AUSTRALIA

Sha

Sha

Colour In

 Szha

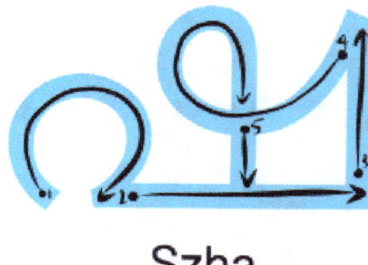 Szha

Colour In

വേഷം Ve-sham Dress

This is traditional Kerala dress- Mundu

Szha ....

Szha ....

Szha ....

LIGHT AUSTRALIA

Sa

Sa

Colour In

സാരി Saree

I love the traditional Indian dress- saree

സ
Sa ....

സ
Sa ....

സ
Sa ....

LIGHT AUSTRALIA

Ha

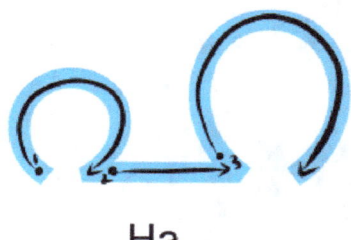
Ha

Colour In

 ....

 ....

 ....

Laa

Laa

Colour In

തവള Tha- va- la Frog

ള ....
Laa

ള ....
Laa

ള ....
Laa

Yza　　　　　　　　　　Yza

Colour In

Ma-zha Rain

I love the rain…

Yza

Yza

Yza

LIGHT AUSTRALIA

 Ra

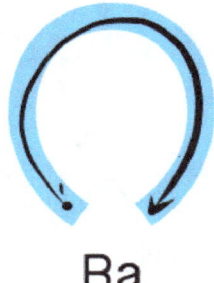 Ra

Colour In

റയിൻബോ Rainbow

Rainbow Rulzzz

Ra . . . .

Ra . . . .

Ra . . . .

LIGHT AUSTRALIA

TO MY WONDERFUL
NEVA & AIDEN

First published by LIGHT AUSTRALIA in 2022

Text and Illustrations copyright (c) Dr. Abraham Thomas, 2022.

Dr. Abraham Thomas asserts his moral rights as the author and illustrator of this book.

Design and Layout by: Facebook.com/Grafixo

All rights reserved. Without limiting the rights under copyright reserved above, no part of this publication may be reproduced, stored in or introduced into a database and retrieval system or transmitted in any form or any means (electronic, mechanical, photocopying, recording or otherwise) without the prior written permission of the author, unless specifically permitted under the Australian Copyright Act 1968 as amended.

ISBN 978-0-6452947-8-1

The illustrations of this book is created with digital art by Dr. Abraham Thomas Eettickal in India | April 2022.

NATIONAL LIBRARY OF AUSTRALIA

A catalogue record of this book is available from the National Library of Australia